STAY TOONED

CARTOONS BY

RHONDA
DICKSION

The Naiad Press, Inc.
1993

Copyright © 1993 by Rhonda Dicksion

All rights reserved. No part of this book may be reproduced
or transmitted in any form or by any means, electronic or
mechanical, including photocopying, without permission in writing
from the publisher.

Printed in the United States of America on acid-free paper
First Edition

Cover design by Pat Tong and Bonnie Liss
    (Phoenix Graphics)
Typeset by Sandi Stancil

Library of Congress Cataloging-in-Publication Data

Dicksion, Rhonda, 1959–
    Stay tooned / by Rhonda Dicksion.
        p.   cm.
    ISBN 1-56280-045-0
    1. Lesbians—Caricatures and cartoons.   2. American wit and humor.
Pictorial.   I. Title.
NC1429.D45A4   1993
741.5'973—dc20   93-4913
                                                                        CIP

DEDICATION

This book is dedicated to the ones I love.
If you make me laugh, you qualify.

ACKNOWLEDGEMENTS

No book would be complete without acknowledging all the little people who make it possible. With apologies to some unsung heroes like the nice lady at the copy machine place, I'd like to thank the following:

The editors and crew at The Lesbian News, Out Front, The Washington Blade, The Weekly News, The Lesbian and Gay News-Telegraph, The Seattle Gay News, Lesbian Contradiction, Chicago Outlines, Deneuve, (the late) El Paso Style, Gaybeat, Gay Comix, Island Lifestyle, Lambda Book Report, Out, and The Lesbian Resource Center Community News.

Magic, for reminding me to take time to stop and pet the puppies.

Barbara Grier at Naiad Press for her delightfully wicked sense of humor.

Most of all, thanks to my partner, Krysta Gibson, for *being* delightfully wicked.

INTRODUCTION

One of the questions I am asked most frequently (besides "May I show you to the door?") is "Where do you get the ideas for your cartoons?" A famous writing instructor once said that the more you try to control your mind the more chaos erupts, so I guess you could say that some of my ideas are the result of an extremely controlled mind.

Anyone who's at all creative will tell you, though, that what inspires them is what they are closest to — the people and places they see everyday. According to my partner, my cartoons are no exception. In private, I am told, she will gleefully admit to a confidante that it takes no longer than 20 minutes, tops, for something she says to pass from her lips to my pen. In my presence, however, the same admission packs enough guilt to get me to sign over my royalty checks.

My partner and I do share an engaging, comical relationship which *may* contribute to my cartoon file. (The two of us are something like a cross between Lucy and Ethel and Thelma and Louise. I won't tell you who is whom, though she probably would.) We live in the country and the sacred cows of humor graze freely around our little homestead. It's a classic case of art imitating life. Two German Shepherds (dogs) and an odd assortment (or an assortment of odd) cats round out the family. In the tradition of the great ranches of the West, we've named our little haven. We call it "The Asylum."

I do most of my cartoons, as I am writing this now, in an old overstuffed blue swivel chair that I inherited long ago from some musty relationship. Like most things that are worth having, this chair is plain, familiar, and comfortable. I like to think my cartoons are like that (except the plain part, of course), so I invite you to pull up your favorite old chair and have a few giggles.

Thanks for letting me into your brain. I promise not to do too much damage, or do any rewiring — I'll leave that to your ex-lover. In *Stay Tooned* I'd like to share some of the stories and circumstances behind a few of my cartoons. My partner may decide to spank me for doing so, but I figure that would be to my benefit — and I might just get a cartoon out of it.

LESBIAN SURVIVAL HINT #230:
IT'S NATURAL TO MAKE A FEW MISTAKES
WHEN YOU FIRST COME OUT.

LESBIAN SURVIVAL HINT #195:
AS YOU SOW, SO SHALL YOU WEEP.

LESBIAN SURVIVAL HINT #164:
THE SUCCESSFUL SINGLE WOMAN ALWAYS
HAS UP-TO-DATE PICKUP LINES.

4

LESBIAN SURVIVAL HINT #179:
THE TIME TO START WORRYING
IS WHEN SHE DOESN'T.

LESBIAN SURVIVAL HINT #211:
WHEN THE TIME IS RIGHT
TO COME OUT, YOU'LL KNOW.

LESBIAN SURVIVAL HINT #159:
SOME OF THE BEST LOVERS
ARE WOMEN OF SIGHS.

LESBIAN SURVIVAL HINT #177:
IT'S A RARE DYKE WHO DOESN'T RESORT
TO A LITTLE BRIBERY NOW AND THEN.

LESBIAN SURVIVAL HINT #193:
THE FOUR STAGES OF THE
LESBIAN LOVE AFFAIR ARE EASILY
RECORDED BY HER TEDDY BEAR.

LESBIAN SURVIVAL HINT #112:
IF YOU BUILD ONE, THEY WILL COME.

EROTICA

I like being in a world where it's so easy to find lesbian and gay erotica. If you live near a major city, you can probably find a place to purchase it. If you're a little on the shy side, you can put a bag over your head, disguise your voice, and order by phone.

I'm fond of lesbian erotica — my partner and I have a few videos which we enjoy watching now and again when we want to spice things up — but some of it seems just a little far-fetched, don't you think? I recently began reading a book of erotic short stories. In the first ten pages the main characters had sex at home, went out to dinner and had sex at the restaurant, and then had sex in an alley on their way back home for more sex. It's never just any sex that these hot heroines have, either. It's the eye-popping, memory-for-a-lifetime kind. It's the kind of sex that makes nuns weep. Oh, please. My partner and I enjoy a healthy sex life, but if those books and videos are to believed, we may as well turn in our lesbian membership cards.

Just once, I want to read a book of erotica that's full of true-life sex scenes. I'd like to see videos about sex that we can all relate to. I'd like to see a story about two lesbians who are nude sunbathing in the back yard, beginning to make love, when they hear their straight neighbors hallooing them from the front yard. How about a story of a planned night of passion with candles, incense, and soft music at the ready, when a cat throws up on the sheets? Maybe even a story where the two main characters have sex a single time then get up and watch television?

I doubt I'll read those stories any time soon. Until then, I'll just have to draw them.

ARTSY BOOKS ALWAYS MADE GAYLE AND
ABBY FEEL SOMEHOW INADEQUATE.

LESBIAN SURVIVAL HINT #168:
SOME SPECIES OF GAY PRIDE
FLOWER BEST IN INDIRECT LIGHT.

LESBIAN SURVIVAL HINT #190:
SOME WOMEN JUST CAN'T RESIST
ADVERTISING THEIR VIRTUES.

LESBIAN SURVIVAL HINT #136:
THERE'S ONLY ONE WAY THAT SO MUCH
HARD WORK AND ATTENTION TO DETAIL
CAN BE PULLED OFF UNDER
SUCH TIGHT DEADLINES.

LESBIAN SURVIVAL HINT #127:
FIRST DATES CAN BE ROUGH

LESBIAN SURVIVAL HINT #138:
"THE SWEET SMELL OF SUCCESS"
HAS A VERY DIFFERENT AROMA
TO LESBIANS ON THE LAND.

LESBIAN SURVIVAL HINT #257:
IT'S NEVER TOO EARLY TO PREPARE FOR
THE SUMMER WOMEN'S MUSIC FESTIVALS.

LESBIAN SURVIVAL HINT #221:
TO LEARN THE LESBIAN LANGUAGE
ONE MUST START WITH THE VOWELS.

FEARS

We all have fears. When you are little, you have silly, little fears, like being afraid of the crocodiles that live under your bed at night, or of being whisked off by those monkey-things from *The Wizard of Oz*. When we become adults, our fears become more grounded in reality. I am afraid of aliens.

I am hesitant to admit this fear — not because I may sound foolish, but because the aliens might hear my admission. That would give them a psychological advantage. I am not sure why I am scared, excepting the fact that I would make a hearty meal for a clutch of them. While others might thrill at the prospect of a tete-a-tete with extraterrestrials, I am terrified. I am convinced that should I be called on to exercise my innate tact, poise, and witty repartè with beings from outer space, the imminent doom of planet earth would be sealed. That would make me feel just awful.

I believe it is important to note that aliens are not to be feared during the day. Aliens shun the light of day, but at night the skies are teeming with them. During the day you may hear a noise on the roof and be able to pass it off as cats playing. At night, that same sound may well be aliens trying to tear the shingles off to get to you.

My partner thinks all this is just hysterical, particularly as she hold with the New Age view that "Aliens are our friends." This is difficult for me to accept. I have coffee with my friends. I call my friends on the phone. I drive my friends to the auto mechanic. In return, I do not expect my friends to take me to another planet, serve me on a platter with toast points, or chase my car down a lonely road at night. This is, however, behavior I might consider typical from some of my partner's New Age friends. All of which led me to the next cartoon...

LESBIAN SURVIVAL HINT #222:
YOU MAY NEVER GET USED TO HER FRIENDS.

LESBIAN SURVIVAL HINT #226:
AT SOME TIME, NEARLY EVERY LESBIAN
WILL HAVE A CLOSE ENCOUNTER.

LESBIAN SURVIVAL HINT #145:
SOME WOMEN WILL STOP AT
NOTHING TO ATTRACT LESBIANS.

LESBIAN SURVIVAL HINT #232:
YOU'LL NEVER BE SORRY
THAT YOU CAPTURED THOSE PRECIOUS
FAMILY MOMENTS ON FILM.

LESBIAN SURVIVAL HINT #120:
UNFORTUNATELY, THERE ARE STILL
SOME THINGS LESBIANS HAVE TO DO
BEHIND CLOSED DOORS.

LESBIAN SURVIVAL HINT #196:
MARRIAGE REQUIRES LOVE, TRUST,
AND SHARING (THE MUFFIN TINS,
THE RECLINER, THE ESPRESSO MAKER...)

LESBIAN SURVIVAL HINT #165:
THE HOLIDAYS CAN BE A
SURPRISING TIME FOR LESBIANS.

LESBIAN SURVIVAL HINT #204:
IF YOU CAN'T BE AN EXPERT, YOU CAN
AT LEAST SOUND UNINTELLIGIBLE.

LESBIAN SURVIVAL HINT #147:
SOME BUREAUCRATIC MISTAKES
CAN NEVER BE RECTIFIED.

43

LESBIAN SURVIVAL HINT #219:
YOUR VIGILANCE CAN SAVE A LIFE.

LESBIAN SURVIVAL HINT #238:
WATCH OUT FOR LITTLE PITCHERS
WITH BIG EARS.

BEING AMAZON

Being a lesbian is not without its priviledges. One of them is the right to wear the title "Amazon." This title allows us to claim knowledge of things not privy to our non-amazon sisters, such as plumbing, auto mechanics, and small appliance repair, to name a few. In the years since I have declared myself an amazon, I have learned that the best way to approach any household or outdoor problem is the same way the expensive professionals do: with a tool of some kind in one hand, a steely glint of determination in my eye, and absolutely no idea what I'm doing.

I usually do get the job done, though. That's why I can say with pride that I have erected a barn, built sheds, managed horses, put up fencing, worked on cars, installed electrical, done masonry, remodeled a basement, fixed an oven, and — the most terrifying project of all — hooked-up a home entertainment system. The work may be difficult or daunting, but I have found that a job well accomplished is its own reward — and if you complain loudly enough while doing it, someone will usually cook dinner for you.

A few years ago, my partner and I decided to move slightly out of the city, to a rural area where there is more room and less activity. We searched the want ads for a place, and hit upon a small mobile home on four and a half acres in a secluded area. Since the rent was right in our price range (next to nothing) there were many other people swarming over the property when we arrived to look it over.

We must have looked especially responsible that day — or it was the bag of dollar bills we had brought with us — because one of the owners took us aside to tell us that she really wanted to rent the house to us, but her husband had reservations about renting to two women. "My husband thinks that two women living here, you know, would call us every time a lightbulb needs changing." I saw her glance around at the scruffy ensemble of hill-folk and drifters who were also hoping to get the rental. Another group was arriving in a hand-painted Gremlin. "I'm going to talk to my husband and see if I can't change his mind," she added quickly.

We later found out that the former tenant had been a handyman. On the day we went to look at the mobile home, the grass was waist-high, mouldering old cars made the place look like a wrecking yard, and there was enough moss on the house to qualify it as a floral decoration. While the landlady spoke to her husband, we went into amazon-mode. "If we rent this place, the first thing I'm gonna do is prune those apple trees and re-seed that pasture," I said in an overly-loud, confident voice, just within earshot of our prospective landlords. "Yeah," my partner replied, "while we're at it we may as well run a conduit out there to the yard light."

We lived there for three years. We didn't re-seed the pasture or run a conduit, but the yard got mowed regularly, the trees got pruned, we put in flower beds, fixed screens, and scraped the moss off the siding. When we moved — to a place farther out in the country — we met with our landlords to return the keys. The landlady took us aside. "I want to thank you two," she said. "You sure put my husband in his place. He's never going to say *anything* about women being helpless again, and I get to hold this over his head for the rest of his life!"

Score one point for the Amazon Nation.

LESBIAN SURVIVAL HINT #24:
MORE AND MORE FOLKS ARE REALIZING
THAT YOU DON'T MESS WITH A DYKE.

LESBIAN SURVIVAL HINT #163:
AFTER SEEING LESBIANS ON DAYTIME TV,
YOU MAY FIND IT HARD TO BELIEVE
YOU ARE ONE.

LESBIAN SURVIVAL HINT #174:
THERE'S NO NEED TO BE BASHFUL ABOUT
ATTENDING A SEX TOY PARTY—
THEY'VE BEEN AROUND FOR EONS.

LESBIAN SURVIVAL HINT #150:
IF YOU LOVE SOMEONE, SET THEM FREE.
IF THEY COME BACK,
THEY'RE PROBABLY BROKE.

LESBIAN SURVIVAL HINT #157:
FOR MOST LESBIANS,
THE "COMING" PART IS EASY.
IT'S THE "OUT" PART THAT'S PESKY.

LESBIAN SURVIVAL HINT #228:
NEVER MAKE THREATS WHICH TAKE
EXOTIC BODY PARTS TO KEEP.

LESBIAN SURVIVAL HINT #91:
SOME WOMEN DO THEIR BEST WORK
UNDER DEADLINES.

LESBIAN SURVIVAL HINT #67:
HER FAVORITE SPORT MAY WELL
USE SOME OF THE SAME TERMINOLOGY
AS YOURS.

LESBIAN SURVIVAL HINT #197:
THERE'S ALWAYS ONE SURE-FIRE WAY
TO BRING LESBIANS TOGETHER.

LESBIAN SURVIVAL HINT #181:
YOU CAN ALWAYS COUNT ON LESBIANS
WHEN THE CHIPS ARE DOWN.

LESBIAN SURVIVAL HINT #239:
CONFIDENCE IS WHEN
YOU CAN DO IT IN PUBLIC.

LESBIAN SURVIVAL HINT #202:
WHAT YOU RESIST IS BOUND TO PERSIST.

THE PARADE

There are a few things I never miss. One is watching my partner get dressed in the morning (the "Where's-My-Underwear Polka" is particularly entertaining), and the other is Seattle's Gay Pride Parade. With attendance estimated at 35 to 50 thousand, the Pride Parade is the easiest way to visually sample all that the community had to offer, as it rolls past you like a movable feast.

There are two simple rules to remember when attending the festivities. First, pick your prime piece of real estate early. If you bring a hat or guitar case you can while away the time collecting change from passersby. Secondly, be aggressive. Don't let anyone sit on top of you unless it is by mutual consent.

The Parade begins with a female motorcycle contingent, dykes on bikes, which revs the crowd into a frenzy. (Thanks to these women, I first learned that no two breasts are identical, especially when whipped to-and-fro by the wind). Following this group, is the Grand Marshall, police cars, fire engines, buses, and Seattle's Imperial Court. Then comes everything else imaginable: professional groups, shopping cart drill teams, Western dancers, floats, queer pagans, parent groups, candidates stumping for office, leather, spikes, high heels, blue hair, and feathers. By the time the Parade is over, everyone is sunburned, hoarse, and spent: earmarks of a truly great time.

I guess the thing that impresses me most about the Parade, though, is how everyone gets along so well. Folks that can't stand each other the rest of the year come together in the spirit of happy camaraderie on that one day. For a single afternoon, we are one big, happy, eccentric family. When I sat down in front of my drawing board to do a cartoon about the parade, I wondered: how much more loving and cooperative could it get?...

LESBIAN SURVIVAL HINT #194:
THE GAY PRIDE PARADE HAS A UNIQUE
WAY OF BRINGING FOLKS TOGETHER.

LESBIAN SURVIVAL HINT #143:
IN OUR COMMUNITY,
20/20 HINDSIGHT IS A PASTIME.

73

LESBIAN SURVIVAL HINT #94:
IF SHE'S IN CRISIS A BIT TOO OFTEN,
IT MAY HAVE SOMETHING TO DO
WITH YOUR STYLE OF COMFORTING HER.

LESBIAN SURVIVAL HINT #162:
NEVER FORGET THE SUNSCREEN.

LESBIAN SURVIVAL HINT #199:
THAT RUSH YOU FEEL
MAY NOT ALWAYS BE PASSION.

LESBIAN SURVIVAL HINT #184:
IF YOU KEEP YOUR EYES OPEN, YOU'LL
FIND SURPRISES AROUND EVERY BEND.

CATS

When I was small I used to have dogs as pets. I was a happy child. When I got together with my partner, she introduced me to cats. My whole life changed.

Some people believe that animals should not be "pets." In our household, cats are not pets — they are the undisputed masters, and we are preordained to a life of service to them. The cats constantly remind us of this fact, and correct us should we err.

If my partner and I find ourselves lingering in bed on a Sunday morning, for example, past what the cats have declared is their breakfast hour (6:30 a.m.), they will sit on our faces to cut off our oxygen supply. If we make the mistake of shooing a cat from a chair so that one of us can sit down after a long, hard day, the cat will wander, unruffled, to an adjoining room and throw up. When we rise to take care of the mess, the cat will reclaim the chair.

There are five cats in our household, each with a style, personality, and place uniquely her own. Sashia is the matriarch. She is graceful, poised, and athletic, and will drink water only from a running faucet. The cry "Cat in the sink!" has provided me with an excuse to avoid doing dishes on more than one occasion.

Ree-ree is the optimist. She is sure that someone wants to scratch her belly if she persists long enough. Her favorite times to persist are when I am trying to draw, when my partner and I are otherwise engaged in the bedroom, or when I am blindly groping my way down the hall to the bathroom in the middle of the night. To this end, she has developed an enticing purr which, when she really get rolling, rattles windows and frightens the neighbors.

Sarah is the orphan. Given to us by a gay friend who

could no longer keep her, she takes solace in food. Much as we have tried to comfort her, she will have none of our attention, prefering instead to fill that empty space inside with Friskies.

Munchkin is our special-needs child. She is dark and rotund, and has never entirely trusted any member of the human species. Since she is so shy, we don't actually see her too often and have nicknamed her "Roach." At night she may be glimpsed scurrying from one dark place to another.

Finally, there is Diana: the child, the clown, and my personal nemesis. Diana has never quite made it past kitten stage — a fact which delights my partner and consternates me. Her antics include jumping on my back when I am bent over working, leaping at the curtains and hanging suspended by her claws, shredding up and nesting in a pile of my pencil sketches, and leading the feline attack force into our bedroom at breakfast time. I believe that Diana is in my life to keep my mind off of aliens — though at night she does bear a striking resemblance to Darth Vader.

Despite all this, I get along fairly well with the cats. I have become resigned to my lot as their obedient servant, a human who is a distant secondary-link in the evolutionary chain of the cat. The only thing that really bothers me in relation to the cats is when I can't tell whom my partner is summoning into the bedroom...

LESBIAN SURVIVAL HINT #102:
SOMETIMES IT CAN TEMPTING
TO BECOME "THE EVIL STEPMOTHER."

LESBIAN SURVIVAL HINT #214:
GOOD FOOD ALWAYS BRINGS
GOOD FRIENDS TOGETHER.

LESBIAN SURVIVAL HINT #142:
SOMETIMES JUST FOLLOWING YOUR BLISS
CAN BE A MATTER OF LIFE OR DEBT.

LESBIAN SURVIVAL HINT #186:
A TRIP HOME FOR THE HOLIDAYS
CAN REALLY HELP YOU
AFFIRM YOUR LIFESTYLE.

LESBIAN SURVIVAL HINT #255:
IF YOU'RE EVER STUMPED FOR A
GOOD EXCUSE—RATIONALIZE.

LESBIAN SURVIVAL HINT #153:
TO SOME WOMEN, "THE BIG O"
MAY MEAN "OVERDRIVE."

LESBIAN SURVIVAL HINT #188:
WE HAVE OUR OWN UNIQUE SET
OF IN-LAW PROBLEMS.

LESBIAN SURVIVAL HINT #170:
SOME PEOPLE DON'T NEED
A MAJOR EXCUSE TO PARTY.

LESBIAN SURVIVAL HINT #160:
THE SEARCH FOR THAT PERFECT GIFT
OFTEN TAKES ONE
INTO UNCHARTED TERRITORY.

LESBIAN SURVIVAL HINT #231:
YOU KNOW YOU'RE ON THE ROCKS WHEN
SHE REPLACES THE RED CARPET
TREATMENT WITH THE BLACK DEATH.

EXCUSE ME, ARE WE ARGUING?

I receive lesbian and gay publications from all across the country, and it tickles me to see how we lesbians interact. We're probably one of the most diverse groups of people ever to share anything in common. We call ourselves many different things: lesbian, dyke, amazon, separatist, feminist, sado-masochist, sapphic, women-oriented, and matriarchal. Whoever said that this is the love that dare not speak its own name must have needed a hearing aid.

Overriding all of our differences, though, is our lesbian connectedness. We are all equal in the arms of Sappho, so no matter what our personal beliefs and practices are, we try really hard to get along with one another as sisters.

I've also noticed that the words we've begun to use reflect our desire to peacefully co-exist. Nowadays, instead of "arguing" we "dialogue;" instead of "gossiping" we "network;" and instead of having an all-out brawl, we "facilitate another's growth."

One day, I was thinking about (er, processing) these terms, when it occurred to me to bring a question before my drawing board for consideration. What would it be like if we applied some of these great new words to the grand old game of softball?...

LESBIAN SURVIVAL HINT #6:
WHEN YOU HAVE SEX WITH SOMEONE,
MOST LIKELY YOU'RE HAVING SEX
WITH ALL HER PARTNERS
FOR THE LAST TEN YEARS.

LESBIAN SURVIVAL HINT #47:
NOWADAYS IT'S GETTING MUCH HARDER
TO FIND A MATE WHO WILL HONOR
YOUR NEED FOR CODEPENDENCY.

LESBIAN SURVIVAL HINT #192:
LONG-TERM COUPLES HAVE A CERTAIN
EASY WAY OF BEING TOGETHER.

LESBIAN SURVIVAL HINT #178:
MOST LIKELY, YOUR SEXUAL ORIENTATION
WAS CEMENTED IN YOUR
FORMATIVE YEARS.

LESBIAN SURVIVAL HINT #191:
THERE ARE SOME THINGS THAT ARE
JUST EASIER FOR A DYKE TO DISCUSS.

LESBIAN SURVIVAL HINT #141:
OUTLASTING THE SHELF-LIFE
OF CORN SNAX IS THE ACID-TEST
FOR MANY A RELATIONSHIP.

LESBIAN SURVIVAL HINT #149:
SOME WOMEN FIND GROCERY ADS MORE
TANTALIZING THAN EROTICA.

PROBLEMS IN THE BEDROOM

When my partner and I first got together, we realized that we had a big problem in the bedroom: we didn't have a bed. My partner owned a small futon (a mattress meant to lay on the floor) which presented obvious problems in a household of five cats who vie with each other as to who can drag in the largest, most exotic, live creature. We opted instead to use my single-wide daybed with its trundle.

For those of you who have had the good fortune never to have encountered a trundle, I think you could define a trundle as "a cot with an attitude." I firmly believe that the trundle was designed as a covert offensive weapon by the Soviets prior to the end of the cold war — if one is not careful, a trundle will happily snap off your fingers, maim your pets, or devour small children. Early in our relationship, my partner and I did not know this. We placed the trundle and the daybed side-by-side, to give us a double bed. This worked well for a few weeks, until one night the trundle decided to wander off. We woke up the next morning with our heads on the daybed, feet on the trundle, and bellies grazing the floor in the gap in-between.

We then tied the trundle and the daybed together with string. This proved to be a minor annoyance to the trundle, which happily chewed through its bonds and was once again free for its nightly walk. We replaced the string with heavy rope. Undaunted, the trundle again broke free. I began to believe that only a hawser from the QE2, blessed by the Pope, could restrain this demon trundle. Any night I fully expected it to levitate and shout obscenities at us.

By this time, we were getting desperate. Not only were we not getting much sleep, but it was difficult to do anything else on the bed. One odd movement or shiver of ecstacy would send the trundle shooting across the room to the far wall. This was not a satisfactory arrangement.

Fortunately, a gay friend of ours decided to move across country and offered us his queen-size bed. We almost wept with gratitude. We brought the bed home and set it up (locking the trundle safely away in a storage unit where it couldn't harm itself or others), and that night we slept the sleep of the blessed. The next night it was back to the sleep of the damned. The rails supporting the new bed were broken and we woke up in a heap in the sink hole which had formed in the middle.

Now, My partner and I never do things by halves. Such was the case with our adventure into the wonderful world of pottery. We decided to try making clay pots for fun and instead of buying a handful of clay, we bought ten 25-pound bags. Our clay period lasted two weeks and by the time of the latest bed incident, we owned ten 25-pound adobe bricks.

Being a lesbian means being resourceful, and we hit upon a plan: we took the bed apart, carefully arranged the bags of clay under the rails, and reassembled the bed. To this day we have been able to sleep soundly every night (should we choose).

I am not sorry this escapade happened because the experience gave me some valuable insight that I can share with friends. When a desolate lesbian comes to me confiding that she is having problems in the bedroom, I look at her baggy eyes and tear-stained face and I recognize the symptoms. I then recommend clay.

LESBIAN SURVIVAL HINT #167:
REVENGE IS A DISH BEST SERVED UP
(AT LEAST) TEPID.

MUCH OF OUR LITERATURE IS HELD
TOGETHER BY ONE CRITICAL STAPLE.

LESBIAN SURVIVAL HINT #83:
NOT ONLY IS LOVE BLIND—
BUT SOMETIMES IT CAN'T
HEAR SO WELL, EITHER.

LESBIAN SURVIVAL HINT #134:
WITH THE ADVENT OF LESBIAN PARENTS,
MOM CAN NOW BROADCAST IN STEREO.

LESBIAN SURVIVAL HINT #161:
THERE ARE CERTAIN FIGURES OF SPEECH
WHICH ARE UNWISE TO USE IN A
MONOGOMOUS RELATIONSHIP.

LESBIAN SURVIVAL HINT #151:
NO MATTER WHAT OUR LIFESTYLES ARE,
THE KIDS ARE GOING TO
GO THEIR OWN WAY.

LESBIAN SURVIVAL HINT #183:
SOMETIMES MAINTAINING TRUST
CAN BE A TOUGH JOB.

LESBIAN SURVIVAL HINT #155:
NEVER TEMPT THE FATES.

LESBIAN SURVIVAL HINT #185:
YOU KNOW YOU'RE CLOSE WHEN
SHE SHARES HER DARKEST SECRETS.

HOMO-SEXUALS

A while back I was engaged in a favorite pasttime: watching television. I do not watch TV for pleasure — that would be politically incorrect. Instead, I use television viewing as a basis for condemning the capitalist/consumerist views of the bourgeousie. Now that we've got cable, I can do this on an even broader basis.

Anyhow, on that night I saw a commercial which showed the evolution of our species. I don't recall exactly what the commercial was about, except that for some reason it linked the Neanderthal foot with inflatable tennis shoes. While the voice-over droned on, I found myself musing on Darwinism, wondering where we will go from where we are now.

I thought about the nature of the human race; how we are beings who are constantly evolving — physically, mentally, and spiritually — until someday we will reach the ultimate pinnacle possible for creatures of flesh and bone. Finally, after as much of this heady contemplation as I could manage — about three minutes' worth, just in time for the next show to begin — I decided that if we don't poison ourselves, or burn ourselves to the ground, there is only one logical next step for our evolution to take...

LESBIAN SURVIVAL HINT #169:
CHANCES ARE, YOUR ANTHROPOLOGY
TEACHER ONLY SHOWED YOU A PORTION
OF THE WHOLE DIAGRAM.

A few of the publications of
THE NAIAD PRESS, INC.
P.O. Box 10543 • Tallahassee, Florida 32302
Phone (904) 539-5965
Toll-Free Order Number: 1-800-533-1973
Mail orders welcome. Please include 15% postage.

STAY TOONED by Rhonda Dicksion. 144 pp. Cartoons — 1st collection since *Lesbian Survival Manual.*   ISBN 1-56280-045-0 $9.95

CAR POOL by Karin Kallmaker. 272pp. Lesbians on wheels and then some!   ISBN 1-56280-048-5   9.95

NOT TELLING MOTHER: STORIES FROM A LIFE by Diane Salvatore. 176 pp. Her 3rd novel.   ISBN 1-56280-044-2   9.95

GOBLIN MARKET by Lauren Wright Douglas. 240pp. Fifth Caitlin Reece Mystery.   ISBN 1-56280-047-7   9.95

LONG GOODBYES by Nikki Baker. 256 pp. A Virginia Kelly mystery. 3rd in a series.   ISBN 1-56280-042-6   9.95

FRIENDS AND LOVERS by Jackie Calhoun. 224 pp. Mid-western Lesbian lives and loves.   ISBN 1-56280-041-8   9.95

THE CAT CAME BACK by Hilary Mullins. 208 pp. Highly praised Lesbian novel.   ISBN 1-56280-040-X   9.95

BEHIND CLOSED DOORS by Robbi Sommers. 192 pp. Hot, erotic short stories.   ISBN 1-56280-039-6   9.95

CLAIRE OF THE MOON by Nicole Conn. 192 pp. See the movie — read the book!   ISBN 1-56280-038-8   10.95

SILENT HEART by Claire McNab. 192 pp. Exotic Lesbian romance.   ISBN 1-56280-036-1   9.95

HAPPY ENDINGS by Kate Brandt. 272 pp. Intimate conversations with Lesbian authors.   ISBN 1-56280-050-7   10.95

THE SPY IN QUESTION by Amanda Kyle Williams. 256 pp. 4th spy novel featuring Lesbian agent Madison McGuire.
ISBN 1-56280-037-X   9.95

SAVING GRACE by Jennifer Fulton. 240 pp. Adventure and romantic entanglement.   ISBN 1-56280-051-5   9.95

These are just a few of the many Naiad Press titles — we are the oldest and largest lesbian/feminist publishing company in the world. Please request a complete catalog. We offer personal service; we encourage and welcome direct mail orders from individuals who have limited access to bookstores carrying our publications.